SURGE

SUPERCHARGE YOUR LIFE, BUSINESS & LEGACY

SURGE

SUPERCHARGE YOUR LIFE, BUSINESS & LEGACY

RICHARD LORENZEN

Ainsley&Allen
PUBLISHING

An imprint of Fifth Avenue Brands LLC
45 Rockefeller Plaza
New York, NY 10111

Front Cover Design by Pinsi Lei
Cover Photography by Alice Gi-Young

ISBN-10: 1-946694-08-8
ISBN-13: 978-1-946694-08-9

To my wife, Pinsi Lei. As a CEO, I have to call a lot of shots every day. Some of them are difficult. She has been unwavering in her support of each of those calls and invaluable as an advisor, including holding me to a higher standard on the ones she didn't always agree with!

To my parents, Richard and Christina Lorenzen, for providing me the foundation and always supporting the journey that got me to where I am today.

CONTENTS

WHY I WROTE THIS BOOK

About one year ago from when I am writing this, I stood in front of a high school class for the first time to deliver a speech on entrepreneurship and answer their questions. This was far from my first public speaking engagement. I've spent the past five years speaking at countless business conferences and gatherings for CEOs and entrepreneurs. But this time was different. I had never spoken in front of such a young group before, and I had no idea whether what I had to say was even going to interest them. What happened over that next hour was the beginning of this book.

In total, I was scheduled to speak to five different classes that day at two different public high schools. What became immediately clear in that first classroom was that I fully underestimated the eagerness of these students to learn about how they might become an entrepreneur one day and that many of them had already considered business ideas of their own, but oftentimes were discouraged from entrepreneurship before they even began. The enthusiasm and passion that the students possessed to learn about entrepreneurship was far beyond what I expected. Granted, entrepreneurship has become a more popular career path over the past five to ten years as it has been glamorized by the media and Hollywood movies about Silicon Valley. Nonetheless, what I saw in those classrooms was something much more real and deep than the superficial motivation of a movie or tabloid story.

I knew on that day that giving these speeches a few times a quarter wasn't enough and that there was a message here that needed to reach as many people as possible. This book is for each of those kids as well as the millions of people around the world who think about starting a business every day. This book is a tool for anybody at any age who wants to live a more fulfilling life through starting a business or even accelerating in their current career. This not an academic resource and you will not find all of these ideas in a university textbook. I am also not claiming to know everything about business. This is a guide based on the personal experiences and insights I've gained while building a successful company and life. This is the road map that I've used in my own life.

Entrepreneurs Are Made, Not Born

A hot debate in the entrepreneurship and startup community over the last few years has been whether entrepreneurs are born or entrepreneurs are made. Many iconic entrepreneurs have come down on either side of the argument. With that said, I truly believe that all entrepreneurs are made. It's simply not possible to be born with all of the character traits necessary to thrive as an entrepreneur. You need to develop them through hard work combined with time. I hope this is more encouraging than discouraging. While nobody was truly "born to do this", anybody can develop what it takes to become successful if they put the work in. This is perhaps one of the greatest issues I saw while speaking in classrooms that led me to write this book. Far too many students discarded their dream of becoming a successful business owner before they even began because at some point somewhere they had been conditioned to believe that success as an entrepreneur was out of their reach for reasons such as not being born with certain skills, resources or family connections. This has never been further from the truth than it is today.

One of the points I emphasize often in my talks is that the playing field in life has never been more level. I know many people will argue with me on the various political aspects of this point. But the truth of the matter is that thanks to technology, the Internet and the countless tools it has made available oftentimes for free, it's never been less expensive or complicated to start a business from scratch and successfully grow it. Now that doesn't mean it is easy. In some ways, technology has made it easier, for certain. But in other ways, no matter what tools exist, building a business still, of course, requires putting in the work in order to succeed. With that said, I have never been more optimistic about the opportunity that exists for anybody - at any age- to go into business and successfully pursue whatever dream they have. So do not put it off any longer.

Share your thoughts with me online. I want to hear your goals: #SurgeBook

CHAPTER 1

YOUR LIFE VISION

The two most important days in your life are the day you are born and the day you find out why. –
Mark Twain

Being an entrepreneur is so much more than just having a job. It is a responsibility that extends beyond your traditional 9-5 employment. Entrepreneurship not a job, it is a way of life. Which is why moving forward, I will talk in great detail about the importance of molding your life around your responsibility as an entrepreneur.

Being an entrepreneur needs to be a fluid part of your life, as you will quickly realize that your role as an entrepreneur will start to impact virtually every part of your life—both personal and professional. With this in mind, before you dive any further into your planning and preparation, you need to have a life vision for yourself.

This life vision is a sort of roadmap to your future, it is your detailed, big goal you have for yourself and for the life you will want to live in the future and your role as an entrepreneur is integral in that vision for the future. Your life vision should be so much more than just a long-term goal or milestone. Your life vision is all about the big-picture view of your life.

Your vision isn't just a milestone you want to reach or a box you want to check in your future, it will define who you are, what you are known for, and what accomplishments and experiences you will have in your life. Your vision isn't just what you are doing but *why* you are doing it. The stronger your life vision is, the clearer your roadmap to your future success will be.

Even if you think you "know" what you want out of life in the future, I encourage you to sit down and really write down and map out what your life vision is. Taking the time to do this will set you up for success both in your personal and professional endeavors and help you stay motivated as you work towards a bigger picture.

Creating a Vision for Your Life

Your life vision is the foundation for everything else. Your vision chooses where your life will go, what it will include and it chooses who your friends are.

Create milestones for yourself that will take you through virtually every stage in your life. Think about what life you want to have lived by the age of 20 and then by 30, then 40, and so-on. You should have markers in place so you can say, "by age 40 I want my life to be like...."

When it comes to sitting down and actually creating a life vision for yourself, it is important that you actually write this vision down. You will need a hard copy of your life vision that you can reference whenever you feel as though you are straying off course or need an extra boost. This hard copy of your vision can also come in handy when it comes to planning for your future plans with your business. As an entrepreneur, this detailed life vision should be a valuable tool that you use to grow your business and to continue with your entrepreneurial pursuits. You should *always* be referencing your life vision as you continue to work towards your goals as an entrepreneur.

The first and most important thing that any life vision is that it needs to include what matters in life *to you.* What is the meaning of your life? How do you want to live your life?

Other questions you may want to consider, that can help you craft this vision include:

What do I want more of in life?

Money aside, what do I want out of my career?

What are my secret dreams or passions that others may not know about?

What do I want in a partner?

What do I want my friendships like? What about my familial relationships?

What things would bring more joy to my life?

What are your values?

What issues do you really care about?

What new skills do you want to develop?

What qualities do you wish you had?

What are your talents? How can you use these in your future?

What is the one thing you would most like to accomplish?

Your life vision needs to answer all these questions. The answers may change over time, but you need to start someone and put a marker out there to work towards.

As you start to refine what your life vision is you need to make sure that it includes a number of details. Just because you are driven by your entrepreneurial pursuits it doesn't mean this is the only thing that you need to include in the outline of your life vision. You need to take a multi-faceted approach to creating your life vision and it needs to include details for areas of your life that you feel are important.

For some people this may be health and relationships, for others it may be time and wealth. Your list for your life should be unique to you. Don't include "experiences" in your categories for your life vision if having certain life experiences aren't important to you. Your vision needs to be unique to *you.*

This is different for everyone, but the different categories for *my* life include:

Business
Finances
Physical Health
Mental/Personal Growth
Lifestyle
Relationships/Family
Faith

For me, these are things that make up my perfect life vision. They may not be the categories that make up your perfect life vision, but they are the categories that make up my own personal life vision. Make sure that you are focusing on what you *do want* in your vision, not what you *don't* want.

Remember that creating this life vision may take some time. In order to do it correctly, you will need to reflect on your life and you need to cultivate some vision and perspective on the topic. This is not something that you should take lightly or rush. You really want to reflect on what it will take to create a vision that will inspire you.

Why You Need a Life Vision

Unless you truly understand *why* you need a life vision and *why* it is important to your future success, then you will never be able to actually reach your future vision for yourself. Your vision is important because it shows you where you are headed and where all of the hard work and goal-setting is going to take you. It gives you a big picture look at what all of your work is really for.

One of the best quotes I have ever heard about creating a life vision comes from Jim Rohn who states:

> *If you don't design your own life plan, chances are you fall into someone else's plan.*

This is a really important thing to remember regarding life plans. You may think that you can make it without a life plan, and chances are you are going to survive without one. However, without a plan of your own, you may wake up one day and discover that you have been living a life that someone else wanted and putting in the work to have a life you don't truly want.

Your vision is also an essential component in your goal setting. I talk a great deal about goal setting for entrepreneurial success. With the right vision guiding everything you will find that reaching these goals becomes much easier. Your vision will breathe life into your goals and give them more meaning, while giving you more drive to make them a reality.

When you inevitably face obstacles along the way, whether they are personal or professional, your vision will help you stay focused and keep you moving forward even when challenges arise. It will also give meaning and purpose to what you are doing. Reaching your goals and overcoming hardships become much easier when you have something you believe in and something that excites you as the driving force behind your actions.

You need a life vision if you want to reach your full potential and if you want to have that extra boost of power and drive behind everything you do. Without it, you can still find success, but you will likely not have the vigor and energy behind it to find as much success as you want. Simply put, your vision is your life force.

What is Included in Your Life Vision?

Now that you understand the *why* of creating your life vision, it is time to get down to brass tacks, and talk about the *how*. Creating a life vision for yourself is so much more involved than saying "I want to be a millionaire who owns my own business." The key thing that separates a vision from a goal is that it encompasses all different areas of your life and is a real "vision" that you can have for your future.

Your life vision should be something that you can close your eyes and see coming true. This is why when you write out your life vision you need to be as specific as possible. Your life vision needs to include more than just what you are doing and how much you are making.

It needs to include what *type* of life that you lead and what kinds of people you want to be surrounded by. Think about what you think you are capable of and what you think realistically you could accomplish if you had the right resources at your hands. This is an important part of what is included in your life vision. If you have no scientific background, then "finding a cure for cancer" may not be a realistic accomplishment. It needs to be real and something that given the right motivation and circumstances you could actually achieve.

Think about something that you wish you could change about or contribute to the world when you think about these accomplishments. This doesn't need to be on a global level, it can be small. However, it needs to be significant, even if it is just bringing a new app to the market or helping shoppers in your area of town find the right blouse. Either way it needs to be something that you can change and something that makes you feel proud.

Finally, your life vision should include what you want people to remember about you when you die. What is the legacy you will leave behind? Make sure this is included in your life vision, even if you feel like this "legacy" is a small or simple one.

Elements such as this can make your mapped-out life vision more detailed and more enriching and they can help make your vision more of something that you can really see for yourself in the future.

Moving Forward

Creating a life vision is only half of the battle. While it can take a while to craft the ideal vision for your future, it doesn't mean that after that you are done. In addition to working towards creating this type of life for yourself, you need to have a system in place that helps you review your vision and update some of the goals and milestones that you have along the way.

If you aren't constantly tracking your progress and checking in to see how much progress you are making towards bringing your life vision to fruition, you may accidentally find yourself halfway through your life and nowhere near the original vision you had for yourself.

No matter what your system is, it should become habitual and something that you do no matter what to make sure you are keeping yourself on track. A great life vision is one of the most powerful motivators that you can ever ask for. Use the power of you having your ideal future life as a way to motivate you to make positive changes, reach the goals you have for yourself and make your life vision become a reality. If you can do this, you are well on your way to becoming an accomplished and successful entrepreneur.

CHAPTER 2

GOAL SETTING

What keeps me going is goals. – Muhammad Ali

When I first started my company years ago, I didn't really know as much as I thought I did. I knew I wanted to be successful, I knew what I was good at and I knew I had the work ethic to make it. I had a lot of things that I knew would help me find success as an entrepreneur. I was driven. I was willing to make sacrifices. I was always hungry for more. However, what I didn't know is what my goals were.

Although I have conquered a number of obstacles in my time, I have also made a number of mistakes. While I have a laundry list of things I wish I could go back in time and change, one of the biggest things I wish I had known more about when I started out is goal setting.

The right goals are the foundation to any entrepreneur's success, plain and simple.

In order for a business to succeed, it has to grow. No company ever survived, let alone thrived, by staging stagnant. Unfortunately, growth doesn't come easy. It takes planning, it takes effort, it takes time and it all starts with strong goals.

There is no way around it. Whether you are naturally a goal oriented individual or not, your business needs to be a goal oriented company in order to succeed. Goals are what get you from point A to point B. They are what gets you from managing five clients to seven clients and eventually to 100 clients and beyond.

Goals are so fundamentally important to the success of any business, no matter what industry you may be in or you may be trying to break into. Yet, goal setting is surprisingly absent from many entrepreneur's daily agenda. Without goals you don't have a target to shoot for. You don't have any place to focus all of your hard work and energy towards.

When you shoot archery, you aim at a target, and at that tiny bullseye right in the middle.

Without the bullseye there as your target, what would you aim at?

What would you focus on?

How would you measure your progress?

How would you know what changes to make in order to be better next time?

How would you succeed compared to others?

You wouldn't do any of these things. You would just be shooting into thin air, hoping and assuming that you were getting better at archery. Your target and your goal is everything. It reigns in all of the skills, talent, drive and ambition and helps you focus it in on one thing, until you have mastered that skill, and can move on to the next target.

While you may not enjoy the goal setting process, your goals are the target that your company needs to succeed, measure their success and to win in a competitive market.

Goal setting is a very specific art form and the base of any goal setting strategy always starts with the right goals. If you have the right goals you can get to the right results.

Choosing Your Goals

I don't need to spend an entire chapter convincing you of the importance of goal setting. Understanding *why* goals are needed is a small but important step. However, it is choosing these goals that is truly paramount to your success.

So, how do you choose the right goal for you?

I have found that one of the most important thing to remember is that your goals need to be *your* goals. Don't set goals based on what others are doing or what others think you should do. Your goals need to be specific to what you want to accomplish as an entrepreneur. It doesn't matter how big or how small they may seem to others, they need to be goals that mean something to you and that will motivate you to achieve them.

You don't want to spend a lifetime climbing a ladder against the wrong wall. If you set goals for yourself based on what someone else thinks or says, or set goals that don't truly matter to you, then you are climbing a ladder to nowhere. Yes, you may still reach the goals you set in the end and find some measurable success, but where will these goals have taken you? Not to where you really want to be. Make your own goals so you can reach your own dreams.

You need to take a goal that you feel comfortable with. Take this goal and make it ten times bigger. If your goals aren't so big that they scare you a little, then they probably aren't big enough.

More than that, you need to truly believe in this big goal. You are the only thing hold you back from making and achieving these big accomplishments. Apprehension and negative thinking can act as a barrier to your own success and ability to reach your own level of success.

Instead of starting small, start big and build your plan around this big goal. After all, you will likely surpass your original smaller goals along your way. It needs to be big, yet attainable and something that truly motivates you to turn that goal into a reality.

Narrow in on what you want your goal to be, and then make sure you refine what you have set out for yourself. There are three main components that every professional goal should have. It must be specific, it must be measurable and it must have a deadline.

Specific – *The more specific your goals are the better.*
You need to be crystal clear on what the main objective of this goal is. A generalized or vague goal isn't helpful. It doesn't provide you with the direction you need and it gives you an easy way to cop out of your goal when things get hard. An arrow that hits the corner of the target, isn't the same as a bullseye.

Measurable – *Every goal must be measurable.*
Measurement brings awareness and clarity. The only way to improve on anything is to measure it every single day. Measure your efforts so you can see just how much progress you are making towards your goal. It is the clearest way to determine whether you are on track or need to make some changes.

Deadline – *Goals without deadlines are merely ideas.*
Set a strict deadline for your goal. If you want to see 100 client visits that is great, but 100 client visits in a week is a much different goal than 100 client visits in a year.

You not only need to know what you specifically want to reach as part of your goal, but when you want to reach it.

Every goal you set needs to fit these three criteria. Take every goal you want to set for yourself and make sure that they all possess these three characteristics. From there, you can start determining which goals you want to set for yourself and your company moving forward, but don't just stop at one goal. Have multiple goals.

Your goals need to work together and cover different areas of your life and your business. Be multifaceted with your goals. Have a few big goals in place for your future, but make sure they are the *right* ones.

Maybe you are ambitious and have 85 goals for yourself in the immediate future. That is great, but you need to narrow them down to the ones that are really important to you and that will really take you to that next step or next phase in your life.

Ideally, you should have 10 goals or less. If you are new to goal setting, or just getting started, then you may want to narrow it down to just three goals. Keeping your goals manageable like this can really help you focus in on what you need to do to accomplish them. After all, just setting the goals won't bring them to fruition, you need to have a plan in place to make them a reality.

Creating a Plan

Now that you know *how* to set your goals, you need a plan for how to execute. The right plan is your roadmap. It needs to be detailed and you need to be able to follow it closely. While setbacks, obstacles and trial and error may all require you to tweak this plan along the way.

You need to essentially start with your goal as your ending point and work backwards. You know where you want to be, now what exact steps do you need to get there?

Breakdown your journey towards your goal into the smallest steps possible. These little milestones along the way will help you track your progress and break down your journey towards your goal in smaller, more manageable steps. The smaller the steps, the easier your path to your goal will be.

Determine exactly what steps you need to take in order to reach this goal. This may take some time. You need to do your research in order to detail just what every step will entail. Here are a few ways to help you do this:

Determine what knowledge you need to gain. Chances are, in order to go from where you are to where you want to be, you are going to need to gain a little more knowledge to get there. Whether this is knowledge on your industry, on marketing tactics, on new skills, or on your competition, the more you know, the farther you will go with any goal-reaching plan. Educating yourself needs to not only be an important part of the goal-setting process, but it is something that you need to incorporate into your steps along the way.

Identify what relationships and associations you need. No successful entrepreneur got to where they are today entirely on their own. I know I didn't. You need to identify the relationships and associations that you need to reach your goals. Who can help you along your way? What connections do you need to make? You need to network as much as possible and make as many connections as you can. You also need to find a mentor that has done it before and who can guide you. (I am going to dedicate much more information about mentors later in the book.) Overall, you need to outline what type of connections you are going to need to make moving forward, whether it's relationships with the press, with other entrepreneurs or those in industries that may help boost your own initiatives.

Establish a way to measure your progress. With every actionable step along your journey, there needs to be an included way to measure your progress towards that goal. This will give you time to review and adjust your plan along the way. Breaking down your review and measurement process can help illuminate any challenges that you may be having along the way so that you can adjust your plan as needed before you end up too far in the wrong direction.

Steps like these are vital to helping you execute your plan and eventually reaching your goal. Every day you should be making progress towards these steps you have laid out for yourself, meaning every day you should be making steps towards your goal.

Every morning when you get up, make reviewing or writing out your goals one of the first things you do. Every evening before you go to bed, you need to review your goals and what you have done that day to work towards them. It sounds repetitive and it sounds tedious, but I promise you that this is one of the most efficient and effective ways to stay on track with any goal.

Once you have reached your goal, congratulations, but your job isn't done. You need to immediately setup something new to work towards. The worst thing you can do is become comfortable after finding success. Reaching a goal is good but it shouldn't be good enough. This is the number one problem that I see among entrepreneurs today. They achieve some level of success and they stop being hungry and stop being driven.

Complacency is the biggest threat you have towards your future success. You need a system for yourself to prevent this from happening. You need to reward yourself and immediately look forward towards the next big goal you have in place and the next big dream you are going to conquer.

CHAPTER 3

DEVELOP THE RIGHT HABITS

We become what we repeatedly do. Excellence, then, is not an act, but a habit. – Will Durant

There are many different working parts that go into finding success. Virtually every aspiring entrepreneur can attest to the notion that finding success is a tireless and difficult journey. So how do you reach this level of success? The first step is to become the *type* of person that can reach the level of success that you want to have.

The people who are most successful in this world don't get to that point because they had the perfect business plan or a flawless model for their company. They got to that level of success because they are a specific type of person. It takes a certain type of person to be a truly successful entrepreneur. Just look at some of the biggest entrepreneurs in the world. They aren't exactly your average everyday person. They are extremely driven, have tremendous work ethics, and may even be a bit peculiar.

One of the most poignant examples of this, comes from the stories that many have told about the late Steve Jobs. The famed entrepreneur was infamous for sending emails all during the night at the most bizarre hours. He was always working and his mind was always churning, and he developed a habit of sending ideas about new thoughts and ideas he would have in the middle of the night. It was a defining characteristic of Jobs, and while it may not have been the most endearing of habits for his employees, it was one that helped him get that edge on other entrepreneurs and ultimately be as successful as he was.

While some claim Steve Jobs was a little "outside the box," he was the *type* of person that would reach tremendous success as an entrepreneur, and he of course, ultimately did.

If you want to find success like these individuals, then you need to be the *type* of person who can reach that level of success.

Becoming the Right Type of Entrepreneur

I talk a great deal about goal setting and just how important it is to have big goals in front of you that you can work towards. Goal setting should be consistent, it should be ongoing and above all things it should be habitual. When it comes to finding success in virtually any realm of entrepreneurship, it is important to make sure you are focusing on the little things and that you are developing little habits that will put you ahead of the competition and on a path towards success.

The right habits can make all of the difference when it comes to finding any measure of success. Any entrepreneur can open up a business. However, it is the entrepreneur that does those little things, that has positive habits such as getting up earlier, working later and staying more focused during the day, is the one who is going to be more successful.

One of the biggest rewards of reaching these goals and finding success is the character that it builds along the way. Reaching your goals is never going to be a quick and easy process, but it is going to make you a better person in the long run. If you want to continue to achieve even more success and continue to reach these goals you set for yourself, then you need to be able to grow as a person.

This growth all begins with the habits that you have. Your habits truly can define you as a person. This is why I truly emphasize the importance of forming habits and focusing on who you are as a person, before you focus on reaching other professional endeavors.

Habits can make or break any entrepreneur. Your habits can make you a better business owner and they can make you a better person. Good habits can make you and bad habits can break you. The key is knowing how to develop good habits while subsequently breaking any bad habits that you may have.

How to Break Bad Habits

Before you can start focusing on the right new habits, you need to start by ridding yourself of bad habits. Just as the right good habits can define who you are as a person and make you a better version of yourself, the wrong habits can hold you back and prevent you from being the best person you can be.

Begin by looking at the bad habits in your life and list them. What destructive or poor habits do you find yourself falling back on? What vices do you have? Think of all of these bad habits you have in both your personal and professional life.

This can sometimes be more difficult than it sounds. Many times we develop bad habits because they make life easier or make life *seem* more enjoyable than it is. Most people don't develop a habit of eating when they are stressed because they think it is good for them. They develop this habit because it makes them feel better.

List these habits and start making a concerted effort from removing them from your life and from your daily routine. Start with one at a time. Bad habits can be very difficult to break and if you try to go cold turkey on all of your bad habits at once, you are much more likely to fail, or pick up some even worse habits.

Set a goal for when you want to break these bad habits and work every day on removing them from your life. Some days you will succeed and some days you will fail. It will likely be a longer journey than you want with ups and downs. However, with consistent effort, over time you will find yourself less and less reliant on these old habits, until they truly become a thing of the past.

How to Form New, Better Habits

Once you have rid yourself from your bad habits, you have a nice, new clean slate to work with as a foundation to build your new, more positive habits on. This is where you will really need to start working.

It doesn't necessarily matter what these habits are, but they need to be something that can better you both as a person and an entrepreneur, and something that you can actually stick with. In order for something to be a habitual, it needs to be something that can be repeated each and every day to a point where it becomes routine, to where it becomes part of your life without effort. If your habit is to get up at 5:00 AM so you can do your emails in peace, then you need to get to a point where you are waking up at 5:00 AM naturally without strain.

Setting the habits that work for you is one thing, but actually turning them from actions to habits is a completely different undertaking. There are six main things that every person needs to understand in order to successfully form better habits.

Character

Developing good habits takes character. It is going to be hard, and it's going to take dedication towards doing the *right* thing. Developing good habits means having the character to do what is right, even when it isn't easy. You need to stay focused on doing the right thing, even when it's hard, in order to develop the positive habits that can change your life and change your future.

Developing new habits doesn't just require character either, it will also help build more character as well. The more dedicated you become towards changing the way you do things and changing yourself for the better, the more character you will build. Chances are you will face adversity during your quest to develop new, permanent and lasting habits you can going to face some challenges along the way. These challenges can be difficult, but they can help build more character in the long run and make you a stronger, more well-rounded entrepreneur in the future.

Discipline

One of the biggest components of successfully developing good habits is to have discipline. It is not easy to change your own natural way of doing things. This is not something that is easy and it is not something that happens overnight. You need to be disciplined in order to make these changes happen. This means making a plan of how to change and sticking to it, no matter how hard it is.

This all comes down to having self-discipline. This means following your mind instead of your feelings. No matter what you feel in a moment, you need to be able to stop and think about the bigger picture and think about what the *right* thing to do is. This often means having the discipline to ignore what you may think you *want* to do and instead do what you *should.*

When you are trying to diet and are tempted to break it with an indulgent piece of cake, saying "no" is having discipline. You need to put this same disciplined approach towards your efforts in forming new habits.

Being disciplined to stick with the new habits you want to form and ignoring the bad habits when they become a temptation can be very difficult, but those who are self-disciplined often find it is much easier to reach their goals.

Sacrifice

If you really want to form new habits that are going to actually stick and actually become part of your everyday routine, then you are going to need to willing to sacrifice a great deal in order to bring these new habits into your life.

This is one of the most difficult challenges that people tend to face when it comes to changing their habits. If you want to form new, better habits that are going to make you a better entrepreneur, then you need to know about and understand sacrifice.

You may need to sacrifice a favorite hobby, a vice or time with your friends in order to form these news habits. It can be difficult, but you need to remind yourself *why* you are doing these things and *why* you need to make sacrifices. In the long run, sacrificing these things in the present will only help you in the future, but it doesn't mean that it is any less difficult.

Persistence

You can't simply decide to form a new habit one day, and expect that it will naturally become part of you. Chances are you will accidentally drop the new habit from time to time, or even accidentally start relying on your old bad habits while you are trying to form new, more positive ones.

Chances are there will also be a time when you are going to feel stagnant in your efforts. Perhaps you started out with great enthusiasm regarding your new habit-forming efforts, and now the initial rush of excitement has faded away. This is normal and it happens to most people who try something new like this. However, if you have persistence then you have what it takes in order to push through and still find success despite feeling like you are bored, stuck, or indifferent to your new attempts to form better habits.

Focus

There are going to be things that get in your way of developing good habits, and this is why sharp focus is so important. You may want to develop the habit of exercising every day after work in order to keep yourself as healthy and energized as possible. However, if other, more fun opportunities come up, you need to have the focus to ignore them and stick to your plan.

Staying focused on what changes you need to make is important, but it is just as important to focus on *why* you need to make those changes. Write out the reason you are developing new habits and use it as a motivation for you to stay focused and stick with your efforts. You aren't just developing a habit of reading 30 minutes a day in order to read more, you are developing that habit for a *reason.* The clearer you are on the big picture, the easier it will be to stay focused along the way.

Reflection

Reflection is a core component of learning and therefore a core component of teaching yourself to form new habits. Reflection is a very natural and very effortless process. You can reflect while you drive home from work or while you are in the shower. Either way it gives you time to think and time to become self-aware.

If you have a strong sense of self-awareness then you can start developing the habits that you need to form to become a better person. Every person is different and every person needs their own unique habits in order to succeed. Use periods of reflection to determine what you need to change about your current habits and what you need to do or change in order to be the best person and the best entrepreneur you can be.

It takes a long time for an action to become habitual. However, with some diligence, focus, hard-work and dedication you can start eradicating those bad habits from your life and replacing them with the positive ones that you need. In the end, these little habits and these little every-day actions are going to be what ultimately changes who you are as a person and who you become as an entrepreneur.

CHAPTER 4

KEEP YOUR MIND AT PEAK PERFORMANCE

Formal education will make you a living; self-education will make you a fortune. – Jim Rohn

I truly believe that much success in entrepreneurship comes from *who* you are as a person. If you want to be a successful entrepreneur then you need to have the skills, the talent and the work ethic, of course, but you also need to have a certain amount of intelligence. This is something that I tell pretty much anyone who will listen, yet it is something that a lot of aspiring entrepreneurs don't want to hear.

If you want to be successful in today's market and you want to thrive as an entrepreneur, then you need to be intelligent. Some people are naturally born more intelligent than others. It isn't a fun fact, but it is a fact. However, this doesn't mean that there aren't things you can do to train your mind and to keep it at peak performance.

If there is one hard, steadfast rule that I have for any aspiring entrepreneur it is this: **Never stop learning.**

If you want to be the best in the business, then you need to constantly be learning and teaching yourself new things. The sharper you are and the more you are able to keep your mind at peak performance the better you are going to perform. One of the great things about training your mind is that you can always be doing something to keep your mind in its top working order.

When your brain is working at peak performance you will not only find that you have the knowledge you need to make better, more informed decisions but you will find that you have the drive and the focus you need to succeed as well.

When it comes to training your mind, I believe in finding certain practices that work best for you and the way that you learn and think. Perhaps you enjoy listening to motivational tapes or reading books from your mentors every morning, or maybe you prefer to attend conferences in person. No matter how it is that you prefer to learn, there are a few ways that you can get started with your mental training.

Use these approaches as a foundation until you build the type of mental fortitude that you need. Remember, this is an ongoing effort. You need to constantly be training your mind each and every day in order to stay at your peak performance.

Read Constantly and Listen to Audio Programs

The more you read, the better off you are going to be. This is part of constantly learning and inundating yourself with as much knowledge as possible. How do you do this? Read, read, read. I cannot emphasize reading enough. You should be reading every single day. If you think you read a lot now, start reading even more.

Reading the news is important, and it is something that I will address a little later on. However, in addition to reading the news you need to read the opinions of those that are real tastemakers in your industry. Read their blogs, read interviews with them and read their books. The more information that you can gather and absorb on tactics, approaches, other people's stories, motivation, and anything in between—the more poised you are going to be to find the success you want to have.

It is important to note that some people may not be visual learnings and may be more auditory in nature. This is why audio programs, books on tape and news stations are such a great resource for so many and such a powerful way to still get the information that you need.

While all of this information isn't necessarily going to stick permanently, you need to be constantly filling your mind with as much information from the outside world as you can. This is one of the best ways for you to grow and to educate yourself. Some of your knowledge will come from your experiences in the outside world, but even more will come from the information that you seek out and read on your own.

Doing this daily is like exercise for your mind. It will train you to absorb information faster and better than ever before, and it will help you keep your mind sharp, quick and accurate.

Review Your Goals Twice Daily

I am such a firm believer in reviewing your goals. In fact, I have an entire chapter dedicated towards goal setting. If you want to keep your mind sharp and focused on what it is that you need to achieve, then you need to start reviewing your goals daily.

Write down the goals that you have and put them in a place where you can see them. Twice a day, take a few moments to read over your goals. Imagine them being achieved. Visualize them coming true. While it may seem like a silly exercise, I promise you that visualization works. You need to really picture a future where your big dreams and goals have come true.

Think about what this looks like. What is your life like now that these dreams have come to fruition? What has changed? Visualize in as much detail as you can about what this life will look like. It is one of the best ways to prepare yourself mentally to reach your goals and to help yourself stay focused on what you need to do in order to make these dreams come true in the future.

I want to stress the importance of doing this twice a day. While some people will start their morning or end their evenings going over their goals, making this an integral part of your life, two times per day is only going to help your goals seem more real and more obtainable.

Practice Constantly

Practice makes perfect, right? Well if you want to stay sharp, you need to constantly be practicing your skills. It is one of the best ways to keep your mind at a peak performance level and it is something that will more than pay off in the end. You need to be practicing the skills that are going to directly impact your business.

For example, if you are doing public screenings every week as your main way to get new clients, you need to practice your elevator pitch. If you are giving public speeches to build your personal brand, practice your speaking skills. If you are a massage therapist giving free 15 minute sessions, practice you massage skills.

Practicing and honing your skills each and every day is paramount to you being the best version of yourself that you can be. After all, you need to be the best in the business, or at least make a case for yourself as the best in the business if you want to find success as an entrepreneur. Doing this means practicing your skills as much as possible so you can become the most talented version of yourself that you can be.

Stay Informed

Staying informed about the world around you is something that really goes hand-in-hand with daily reading, but I want to make sure that you emphasize staying informed even outside of your daily reading habits. The more up-to-date you are with the outside world and to topics relevant to your professional endeavors, the better off you will be.

You need to be reading about topics in your industry. Read articles and blog posts from those you admire in your industry. Read the news. Read about market trends. There is no better way to fill your brain with information.

I want you to stay informed about these relevant topics whether you read a certain section of the paper every morning or if you have a news ticker feed rolling across the top of your screen. It is important to hone in on topics that are only relevant to you and your industry, and I say this because you don't want to become too overwhelmed with information overload.

In most situations, celebrity news and gossip isn't going to fit in with your "realm" but it also doesn't mean that you only need to focus on news stories directly related to your business. Stay up-to-date on market trends, news related to small businesses, local laws that may impact your company and even marketing and advertising trends. If it is news that will help you grow your company, you need to be reading or listening to it.

Always Focus on Gratitude and Abundance

There are a number of things that you can do in order to train and strengthen your mind and stay in peak performance mode. However, just as positive things can help strengthen your mind, negative things can have the reverse effect on your mental fortitude.

You need to banish negative thoughts from your mind. Once you have those negative thoughts in there, they can eat away at you and all you have worked for. The best way to kill these negative thoughts is to focus on the positive.

Be grateful for the positive things that you have in your life. Address the things in your life that you are lucky to have and express the gratitude that you have for them. This will help you stay focused on being happy with what you have and what you have achieved, even when life throws you some curve balls.

This can be a difficult mindset to have and to maintain, but I promise you if you talk to today's most successful entrepreneurs, they know how important this positive way of thinking is. This approach is one that can not only help keep negative thoughts at bay and keep you performing to the best of your ability, but it is one that will help you learn to value and truly appreciate all that you have worked for and accomplished during your journey.

Above all things, a positive mind is a sign of a strong mind.

Reflect Every Evening

Your morning routine is really important. In fact, so many of the best minds in the industry claim that one of the keys to success is getting up and getting your day started on the right foot. Yes, this is important, but it is just as important to make sure that you have an evening routine in place as well.

Make reflection part of your evening routine. At a time when most people are zoning out and winding down for the night, focus on reflection. It will give you that mental edge you are looking for and help you stay in peak performance mode.

Reflection is best done by asking questions. I want you to go over the following questions with yourself every evening:

What did you learn today?

What can you improve upon for tomorrow?

What were your wins and losses for the day?

Answer these questions as honestly and as accurately as you can. I even know some people who like to write them down so they can go back and look at the progress they have made over time. I truly believe that reflection is one of the best ways to hold yourself accountable and to make sure that you aren't accidentally slipping.

Self-reflection will keep you focused on your goals, focused on your progress and realistic about how your performance is going. While you may think that the end of the day is a time to relax and unwind. I challenge you to start reflecting every night, just give it a month. I promise that with time you will start to see a significant change in your own focus and your own ability to stay on track with your goals.

A sharp brain and strong mental focus are some of the most powerful tools that you have when it comes to establishing yourself as an entrepreneur. If you have made it this far, you have the type of mind that is needed to really establish yourself as a successful entrepreneur, but you need to make sure that you are keeping your mind as healthy and as powerful as possible.

You may have the natural talent to be a professional athlete, but if you never practice or workout, you won't be the best athlete you can be. Never undervalue the strength of your own mind and make sure that you are working every day to keep your mind in its optimal peak performance.

CHAPTER 5

AVOID INFORMATION OVERLOAD

What controls your attention, controls your life. –
Darren Hardy

There are so many ways we can gather information from the world around us today, and in many situations, especially when creating your own company, information can be a powerful tool. However, there is such a thing as too much information, or the infamous term "information overload." It is a term that is used to describe the constant bombardment of information that comes from tweets, texts, emails, articles, Facebook posts, viral videos, Snapchats, and more. It is an exhausting amount of information that can flood the mind and does anything but help you be productive. The problem isn't just in the digital realm either. Look at grocery stores, clothing retailers, soda machines. It seems that virtually every aspect of our lives today is filled with choices and with options and with an overwhelming amount of "things" that can only clog our minds.

This is what information overload is and while it may not seem like that big of a deal, it can be one of the biggest distractions to any entrepreneur. The average brain can only pay attention to around three things as once. When the brain starts to become overwhelmed from attempting to focus on too many things at once, you can start to lose your focus. Losing focus is one of the worst things that can happen to any entrepreneur looking to build up their business.

With this in mind, I always encourage every aspiring entrepreneur to think about the amount of information that they are flooding their brains with. Before you go any further with building your company or trying to put in the work needed to grow your new business, you need to "clear out the clutter" so to speak, from your brain. Avoid information overload and you can get the crystal-clear focus you need to reach your goals and find the success that you want.

So, how exactly do you do this in an information-driven world? There are three main ways that you can still get the information that you need in our digital age while avoiding information overload.

1. Stay informed only of relevant information.
2. Focus on the information relevant to your goals.
3. Cut out garbage input.

If you can do these three things, you will find your mind is clearer, you are more focused and that you are going to be much more productive during your day. There is a serious issue that impacts so many of us today, and it is simply called analysis paralysis. It is when you have so many options, opinions and pieces of conflicting information coming your way that your brain freezes. This information overload can put you into a paralyzed state of inaction, and when you are in this state, you tend to lose up to 75% of the information that you think you are taking in.

This means while you may feel overwhelmed, but insist on pushing through and trying to take in this information anyway, your efforts may be futile and you may just be wasting your time as you absorb only ¼ of what you think you are reading. This is why it is so important to focus on the *right* information and push the *wrong* information to the side. If you can learn how to do this, I promise you it will be one of the most valuable tools that you learn as an entrepreneur.

What Information Should You Be Focusing On

In today's day and age, there is a ton of information that you need to sift through during your everyday life. Some of this information is good, some of it is bad and some of it can just get in the way. The first thing that you need to do is to determine *what* information you need to be focusing on. Simply put, your focus should be on what is relevant to you.

The information that you focus on should be relevant to you and your goals. This may not be the same information for everyone. For one person, an article on the Spurs basketball team may be mindless information, but for someone starting their own sports blog, it can be relevant. It is up to you to determine what information you need to be staying relevant on and what information is only getting in your way. It is important that you are honest with yourself about what information is what so you can stay focused on the important things and cut everything else out.

Now, just because your focus is on your success as an entrepreneur it doesn't mean that the information that you take in has to be directly related to your professional endeavors. It can also be about self-improvement, motivation, relationship management or other categories that may be relevant to your overall life vision. The important thing to remember is that you should be clear and honest with yourself regarding what information is really relevant to your life and what information is not.

Stay Informed of Relevant Information

One of the best things about living in this age, especially for entrepreneurs is that you have *so much* access to relevant information, more so than any other generation of entrepreneurs before you. The worldwide web is filled with resources to help you along the way, including blogs, articles and even this eBook. There is information out there that can really help you understand what to expect from your foray into the world of entrepreneurship, and you should use it. However, it is important to find a unique balance of using the web to your advantage without falling victim to information overload.

Studies have been done on the brain's ability to process information. The human mind can only take in so much information at a time. If you cross this threshold and overload your brain with too much information, you are putting yourself at risk for stress and confusion, and in most situations your brain actually starts to tune out a lot of the information you are trying to process while your focus and performance levels begin to drop drastically.

With this in mind, you may think that you can handle an overload of information, or that your brain can easily switch between taking information for work such as reading an article, or this book, and the text message or Facebook post that just came on your phone. This is not true. When your mind is flooded with information, it doesn't matter where it comes from or what you are using it for, there is a point where your brain's ability to focus and process information is going to be impaired.

There is a lot of relevant information out there and you need to be as up-to-date on as possible. This includes information on investments, market trends and things that are happening within your field. This is great information and it is information that you *need* to stay informed on. However, in order to process this information to the best of your ability you need to hone in on the relevant stuff, and cut out the garbage.

This is why you need to really hone in on what information you need to be reading, soaking in and focusing on. When you aren't reading this information, don't overload your brain with even more YouTube videos and funny articles from your favorite blogger. Give your mind time to rest and reset. While it can be tempting to always be locked in to everything around you, if you try to soak up too much at once, your brain may inadvertently take in that celebrity gossip column you read instead of the market research information on your target consumers.

Be diligent about what information you need and what information can actually help you with your professional efforts. The more focused you stay on this information, the more you will actually absorb this relevant information so you can use it later on.

Tips for Cutting Out the Garbage

The hardest part about avoiding information overload is not determining what information is actually relevant, but it is about cutting out the information that is *fun* to take in, but that isn't really relevant to your life and what you want to accomplish as an entrepreneur.

This typically includes things such as junk TV, useless social media, gossip and mindless web surfing. While we are all guilty of indulging in these things from time-to-time and while they can seem harmless enough, they can actually really distract you from what is important.

This is actually a lot harder than it seems, but there are a few tips that you can use to "cut out the garbage" so you can focus on what matters.

Set up a system for yourself.
If you really want to set yourself up for success, then you need to set up a system that will help you cut out the excess noise. This can be something as simple as blocking Facebook notifications from coming from your phone or blocking a website that you like to mindlessly surf on. No matter what parameters you need to keep yourself focused, put them in place. Different people benefit from different systems, so you need to find one that will work for you.

Only follow a few blogs.

Blogs and other relevant resources can be a great way for you to gain tips about your industry or insights on being an entrepreneur. However, no matter what industry you are in, chances are there are a lot of those blogs out there. It can be easy to fall down the rabbit hole into a whole other world when you start to get caught up in these blogs, especially when you start following them daily.

Even though these can be great sources of information, there can be a point where you are just following too many and doing too much. Choose one or two blogs to follow and cut the rest out, chances are this is all you need anyway.

Keep yourself away from certain information sources for at least one day at a time.

Just because you are looking to cut down on information overload, it doesn't mean that you can't access some of your favorite sources of fun information from time-to-time. One great way to make sure that you aren't overdoing it in terms of indulging in this type of information, whether it's mindless television or your favorite sports blog, is to keep yourself away from certain information for a day at a time. Say Tuesday is your day to just not watch TV at all. Giving yourself an entire day to break away from one source of "garbage" information completely will not only give your mind a break for that day, but it may just show you that giving up some of this garbage information is easier than you think.

If you really want to push yourself, then try going on an information cleanse. This means completely stepping away from all of your information for a day or weekend. It may be hard to get used to, but it will have the same effect as a food cleanse and act a "cleaning out" of your mind.

Unplug every day.

You need a moment everyday where you completely unplug from the technology around you. Yes, this is harder than it seems, but it will be really good for you and will help you clear your mind. Even if it is just for 30 minutes, step away from your phone, email, social media accounts, computer, everything. Walk away from these sources of information completely. Go for a walk, relax, cook, work out, no matter what it is, you need to be completely unplugged from the world around you. If you do this, you can give your mind the mental break it needs to refresh and refocus.

Herbert A. Simon once said that a "wealth of information creates a poverty of attention." And in this area, he really is on point. The information that is available to you as an aspiring entrepreneur can be the key to your success, but it can also be the key to your downfall. Don't let information overload lead to productivity issues, lack of focuses or "analysis paralysis." Remember the impact that information overload can have and make the extra effort to avoid it all costs. Adding this extra step into the way that you organize your day can make a dramatic difference in how productive you are able to be.

CHAPTER 6

MANAGE YOUR TIME RUTHLESSLY

The bad news is time flies. The good news is you're the pilot. – Michael Altshuler

If there is one thing that every *type* of entrepreneur without-a-doubt needs to succeed, it would have to be time. Despite all of your other talents and accomplishments, if you don't have the time to commit to your company, then you are never going to reach the level of success that you want to. Unfortunately, there is no way to magically make more time in the day. However, you *can* take some extra steps in order to manage your time better, so that you have more usable and more productive time during your day.

Chances are, at this point in your career, you have heard endless tips on "effective time management." However, I want you to take the time to think differently about the concept of time management. I don't want you to just think about managing your time *better*, I want you to be *ruthless* with your time management. It takes a certain tenacity in order to really change the way that you use your time. It is about being entirely dedicated to transforming your approach to time management.

In order to really see a difference in how you use your time and how much available time you have to dedicate toward your business, then I encourage you to try this three step process that will have you learning to ruthlessly manage your time. I want you to really follow this plan and make sure that you are not wavering from the plan. It takes ruthless determination in order to be ruthless with your time management. Here are the three tips that you can utilize in order to completely change the way you spend your time during the day.

Step 1: Identify

Before you can start managing your time better, you need to identify *what* is most important when it comes to reaching your goals. You must be able to identify the tasks and uses of your time and realize what is the most effective approach for reaching your goals.

You also need to identify the *how* in the equation. Identify *what* you do best and what moves the meter most and helps you get the most done. Make an effort to only do those things. Don't waste your time with tasks that won't quickly move you towards your final goal.

As you start to identify what it is that you need to get done make sure that you are understand the difference between urgent and important. This is one of the key things you need to accomplish in the identifying stage as it will help you later on when you prioritize and plan out the time that you have. Something that is important needs to get done. Something that is urgent needs to get done in a certain timeline.

Identifying what you need to spend your time on is actually more complex than many people assume and it deserves the right amount of time and attention. Part of identifying what you need to do with your time includes being able to delegate tasks. If you want to make the most of your time and get everything important done, then you can't do it all on your own.

As you identify what you need to accomplish, make sure you are also focusing on time. Be realistic with how long everything is going to take. Delineate a time limit on when to complete each task and make sure that it is a realistic time constraint. Having a constraint such as "I'm going to work on this project for four hours," is going to push you to be more efficient and get more done. You should always be "racing against the clock" so to speak, to introduce a sense of urgency into your day.

Even if you eventually need to go back, spend some more time or iron out the details, you need to be able to identify how much time you want to spend on something as you identify what it is that you need to get done.

Step 2: Prioritize

Once you know what the highest value items are for your day, then you need to prioritize your schedule. Many people have heard of one of the golden rules of time management which is to complete the most important tasks first. This is something I want you to remember when you prioritize.

When you prioritize these "important" tasks, there should ideally only be between one and three things that you are focusing on doing. Even if you only get your two important tasks completed, you are still getting two very important things done with your time. In short, your day has already been a success.

When you prioritize, it is important to remember that there is a significant difference between priority and urgency. Once you have prioritized your schedule, you need to stick with it. Don't get easily distracted and don't let distractions take you away from doing what matters most.

It can be difficult to prioritize tasks when you are an entrepreneur, especially when you are just getting started. This is a time where everything seems dire and everything can seem like a top priority. There are a few ways that you can train yourself to be better at prioritizing the tasks on your plate. One of the simplest and most effective approaches I've seen used is as easy as "1, 2, 3," literally.

I want you to categorize everything that you have to do today into one of three categories.

Priority 1: Critical tasks. This is anything that you need to get done right away or something is going to go terribly wrong. This can be getting a proposal done for a potential new client before your meeting.

Priority 2: Everyday business. These are the things that you need to do in order to keep your company running as usual. Everyday business responsibilities can include your daily marketing, sending invoices, ordering products, or whatever you need to keep your company working.

Priority 3: Everything else. This is where busy work comes in, surfing the web, sending those funny cat videos to people, and catching up with friends on Facebook all comes in.

One of the best things about this system is that most days by the time you cover everything in "Priority 1" and "Priority 2" you have hardly any time to get to "Priority 3." If you want to find a way to cut back on the amount of time you spend surfing the web, this is one way to do it. There are going to be days when you don't even make it to everything in the "Priority 2" category. This is when you need to be flexible enough to revamp your time management skills.

Did you not make it to this category because of poor planning? Because of an unexpected emergency? Because you failed to delegate tasks? Is this something that you can do tomorrow, or will it impact our business if it doesn't get done today? When you are learning to prioritize you need to be willing to be flexible while you figure out how to balance everything effectively so *everything* can get done.

Step 3: Plan

In order to better with how you manage your time, you need to be ruthless with your planning. The more you plan, the more effective you will naturally start using your time. You need to do everything you can to plan out as much of your time as possible. This not only means in the short-term, but in the long-term as well.

A lot of people plan their day out that morning or organize their time with a schedule. I want you to take that to the next level. Plan your days in advance the night before. Plan your weeks in advance the weekend before and plan your months and quarter in advance as well. The more you plan, the more diligent you will be in organizing where your time goes each and every day.

One of the trickiest things about time is how easily it can slip through your fingers if you aren't careful. We have all been there before, where we suddenly realize that time has gotten away from us and we can't account for where that time has gone. The more you plan, the less likely this will happen.

Before you go into planning your days, I want to take a moment to talk about sleep. For so many busy entrepreneurs today who are trying to balance everything on their plate, sleep is often the first thing to get cut from their schedule. The mindset of "I can just sleep an hour less to have an hour more of work," doesn't cut it. You need to plan sleep into your schedule and you need to give it the importance that it deserves.

Every person needs between 7-8 hours of sleep per night. Cutting this sleep out will leave you less focused, less energetic and it can cause you to get sick, which will only put you behind with your pursuits. Plan to sleep. Plain and simple. Great time management is a plan that includes plenty of rest every night. No matter how much time you think you are "wasting" while sleeping, this rest may just account for some of the most important hours of your day.

Whether it is sleeping or working on a project, as you plan out your day, make sure that you reference the time constraints that you already identified for your important tasks. Use these time constraints to plan out your day, but make sure that you leave time between each task. This will prevent you from feeling rushed and it will keep you focused and motivated. Having a little down-time to relax, meditate, stretch, walk or just step outside is actually very important and a great way to spend your time.

After you identify, prioritize and plan, you have already set yourself up for success when it comes to using your time during the day. Doing these three things will put you in a position to start getting the most out of the 24 hours that you have during your day. When it is time to actually execute, it is important that you follow through on all of the preparations you have made this far.

When it is time to get a task done, devote all of your focus to completing that task. Close out of your social media accounts, put your phone away and turn off your email notifications. Focus on what you need to get done.

Don't try to explain your lack of attention away on "multi-tasking," or that you are too busy to only do one thing at a time. If you want to be ruthless with your time management and actually get the most out of the minutes that you have in the day, then you need to have this type of focus.

If you are hesitant about adopting this type of laser-focus with your daily responsibilities, I challenge you to try your "multi-tasking" approach one day, as you try to do 100 things at once, and then try a more focused approach the next. I promise you, even though doing one thing at a time can seem tiresome, you will get so much more done if you have the discipline and the diligence to only focus on one thing at a time before moving on to the next.

I truly believe that a strict approach to time management is one of the most effective solutions for getting the most out of your day and out of the time that you have. Keep these three steps in mind as you start to change the way you manage your time. It is going to take a while in order for you to really master the art of effective time management. This is why I always tell people that you need to be ruthless when training yourself to be more efficient with your time.

I promise you with the right amount of planning and focus it will see like you have more hours in the day than you ever have had before.

CHAPTER 7

MY TOP 14 LESSONS FROM EXPERIENCE

A mind that is stretched by a new experience can never go back to its old dimensions. – Oliver Wendell Holmes, Jr.

So many of the insights that I pass on in this book all come from lessons I have learned myself directly-- sometimes the hard way. From those powered by my successes to those influenced by my failures, I am fortunate enough to have a bevy of life experiences that have taught me some of the most crucial lessons about entrepreneurship. Throughout this book, I have delivered both professional insights and personal stories to help illustrate some of these lessons. However, like any busy entrepreneur, I understand that many of you want the short and succinct, down and dirty versions of these lessons that you can skim, interpret and apply to your own journey in today's market.

With this in mind, I have chosen 14 of the most important lessons I have gained from my own experience. These are lessons I believe that any aspiring entrepreneur can learn from and apply to their own lives and their own journey towards success.

1. Action Always Trumps Planning

This is one lesson that I have not only learned in my personal life but my professional one as well. You can spend all of your time planning out every detail for something, but many times, in the end it doesn't matter, because even the best laid plans can go awry.

Instead of spending all of your time planning, take action right away. Sure, you will likely make some mistakes or need to change your course of action over time, but at least you are making progress towards your bigger goals. I always choose progress over perfection.

Instead of spending all of your time planning for every detail of your future endeavors, come up with a simple plan that will get you started and take action. Why waste all of this time planning when you could be spending just as much time doing? This will not only help you save time and get started faster but it will help you learn about the importance of constantly growing, changing and adapting to the market around you; an essential skill for any entrepreneur.

Remember this: you can plan all you want, but there is nothing you can do to change the way the world around you reacts. You must be ready to make changes and ready to throw your old plans to the wayside, otherwise you will never survive. Have an adaptable mindset and a plan that can grow and change with your future, your business and your industry and you are setting yourself up for success. Ditch your long-term planning sessions and take a risk and start taking action. I promise you, once you get over the initial fear, diving in will pay off in the end.

2. You Need Mentors

I talk about mentors a lot. Not only in this book, but in my everyday life and with any person who is just getting started in the business. No successful entrepreneur did it all on their own. They not only had a team of people around them, but they had a mentor, or more likely several mentors, pushing them and guiding them along the way.

There is no better person to turn to for advice than someone who has already done it before. You can learn from their mistakes and you can learn from their successes. You can mimic the things they did right and avoid the things they did wrong. Most importantly, you can look to someone else to see first-hand how it is done.

One of the biggest misconceptions that people have about mentors is that they all need to be an in-person mentors. While it would be nice to have unprecedented access to a mentor who you could go and visit on a whim every time you have a challenge, most mentor and mentee situations are not set up like this.

You need to understand that you can learn from a mentor in a variety of different ways and through a variety of different platforms. So while you may have one or two in-person mentors, you can also learn from some of the best minds in the business without ever having a conversation with them. Read the books and the blogs of entrepreneurs that you emulate. There are so many successful business owners today who are ready and willing to share their stories, their insights and their own experiences with others.

Take advantage of the material that they put out in the world.

No matter how you choose to follow or learn from your mentors, you need to have some in one form or another. It doesn't matter if they are the most traditional mentors, but they need to be someone who has been where you want to go and who you can learn from in one way or another.

3. You Also Need Experts and Advisors

I talk a great deal about how no entrepreneur can find their peak level of success without others to help them along the way. You cannot do everything yourself, you need experts and advisors to help you. More pertinently, you can't make every decision on your own.

While you may know what is best for you or your company in certain situations or scenarios, if you rely only on your decisions you are only limiting yourself and the future of your company. You can't make every decision on your own. You simply don't know enough, and how could you? Not every person is an expert on everything, so you need multiple perspectives and multiple inputs to make the best decisions possible for your organization.

Remember, your own perspective is actually flawed by your lack of experiences and knowledge. This is not to discredit you or your accomplishments, it is to help you realize that you need help filling in the gaps where you may not have as much expertise. Bill Gates, Steve Jobs, Richard Branson, they all knew a lot when they were starting out and even at the peak of their success, but they didn't know everything. The reason they all managed to be so successful is because they had some of the top minds in the world working with them as experts and advisors.

One of the best things you can do is to try to bounce as many strategic decisions as you can off of your more experienced advisors. Maybe they will accept the decision, or reject it, or offer insight on how it can improve, but either way, the right experts and advisors are the most valuable tools that you have. Use them wisely.

This doesn't mean that you need to always blindly follow their advice, or take their recommendations every time, but you should still seek their advice. Sometimes a second opinion can confirm your original notion or make you rethink something all together. This is also a great way to wide your own perspective and vantage point. The more well-rounded your view is, the smarter decisions you will be able to make for the future of your organization.

4. The Only Way to Get Over Fear is With Action

I have already discussed the importance of taking action instead of just focusing on planning. While ditching your detailed plans in order to dive in head first may seem scary or overwhelming, what many people don't realize is that taking action is actually one of the best ways to get over fear.

Being afraid is normal. It is part of life and it is part of being an entrepreneur. However, the best way to get over this fear is by taking action. It is alright to be scared, but you can't talk yourself into not being afraid of something. You can't trick your mind into not being afraid of something, but you can take action and start conquering your fear.

Every time you push yourself to take action, take that next step and face your fear, your tolerance for risk increases and you are removing boundaries and fears that may hold you back. Always keep pushing yourself and pushing those boundaries. It raises your tolerance level for risk and it can help catapult you not only past your fears but on to bigger and better things.

For example, if making a $10,000 investment scares you, you need to do it. It may be hard, it may require some willpower, but you need to take action and do it. You will never just "talk yourself" into not being afraid of this type of risk, but if you take a step and take a risk, you may be surprised to find out just how quickly you can get over it.

Pretty soon, you will be comfortable with making a $20,000 investment and then a $100,000 investment. It is all about getting over that initial fear and conquering it. From there, the possibilities are truly endless to what new hurdles you may be able to take on.

5. Treat Everybody Well

You must treat everyone kindly. Plain and simple. No matter what they have done to you or how you feel about them, the way you treat people has a tremendous impact on your success.

Yes, the old lesson that you mother taught you about treating others the way you want to be treated is actually one of the most prevalent lessons that you can apply to your experience as an entrepreneur. No matter how much success you have had as an entrepreneur, if you stop treating people well, you have lost everything. Your ability to treat people the right way will always help you in your journey whether you are just getting started or are the most successful entrepreneur on the planet.

It does not matter who a person is, what they do, or how good or bad their own attitude is. You need to treat everyone you meet with kindness. It is not only the right thing to do, but you never know who may be your next client or customer, or your next partner.

You also never know what reputation your brand and your name may earn, based on the way that you treat people. You wouldn't want all of your hard work in building your brand to go to waste just because you were rude to someone.

It can not only help you along your journey and in your efforts to network, get new clients and make new business relationships, but it is also good karma. What you put out into the world will come back to you, so make sure that you put the right attitude out there. You never know what type of positive impact it may have on your company in the future.

When all of your work is over, and you are done with your career, all you will have left is the legacy that you leave on this earth. Make sure that you leave the right legacy behind. This all starts with treating every person that you meet the right way.

6. Build a Personal Brand

When you start a company, it needs to have its own unique brand identity. This is essential to giving your company the unique personality that it needs to stand out in the market. However, in additional to developing a professional brand, you also need to make sure that you create a personal brand for yourself. Every entrepreneur needs this. You need to be as identifiable on your own as your company is.

In addition to knowing what your company is and what it does, the public needs to know who you are and what you do. While these brand identities can share certain traits and aspects, and even intersect at times, they need to be separate. You never know what will happen to your company and its reputation, but if you have a strong personal reputation to fall back on, you are setting yourself up for long-term success.

I want every entrepreneur to remember to give their personal brand the time and attention that it needs. Do not make the mistake of neglecting your personal brand just to focus on and build your company's brand. While you may need to give more nurturing and attention to a growing company brand, you still need to dedicate plenty of time to your personal brand. One cannot thrive without the other. You need to have both.

This is not only important for creating and growing your company, it is important for the aftermath of building your business. Once you sell your company, you are going to need a brand identity for yourself. Once your company is gone, you still need to make a marketable identity. Branding yourself is something that can lead you to a lifetime of success.

Your personal brand will be a valuable asset throughout your entire life and your entire career. You may think that you will own your business until the day you retire, but you never know what life will throw at you (I've already discussed the importance of over-planning and under acting). No matter what obstacles life throws at you, having a strong personal brand can help you through any situation, whether good or bad.

7. Become a Great Salesperson

It doesn't matter what your official title or role is, or if you aren't a "sales" person, if you want to be a successful entrepreneur, you first have to be a great salesperson. Everyone in life is a salesperson in one respect or another. Whether you are selling yourself to your client or your boss, selling a product to a client, or selling your idea for a company to the public, you need to adopt a sales-mindset if you want to succeed.

The level of success that you ultimately reach is directly correlated to how well you can sell. As a business owner you are going to need to be able to constantly sell your ideas, sell your company and sell yourself, whether it's to a customer, network connection or an investor. If you aren't particularly good at sales, now is the time to learn.

Read sales books, attend seminars, listen to audio speeches, follow blogs, study the greats. Do whatever you can to learn the art of sales. It may not seem particularly important to you at a time when you are trying to build your company, but it can make all of the difference in the world in how quickly your company grows and how much lasting success you are able to find. There are so many proficient sales experts out there and so many of them are willing to teach others how to master the art of the sale. Learn from them. Put them on your list of mentors. No matter what it takes, you need to start learning how to sell.

You not only need to be able to learn how to sell but you need to start really honing that skill. Practice your sales pitch all the time, work on techniques even if you are just selling your girlfriend on a new place to eat. Practice, practice, practice so that sales becomes a second language to you.

If you look at any successful entrepreneur today, whether they wanted to be in sales or not, chances are they are now a proficient sales person. If you can sell yourself as an entrepreneur and sell your company with real conviction, you are already a leg up on your competition.

8. Keep Your Momentum

This is a hard lesson to learn, but an important one, and one that I will always carry with me. If you want to not only find success, but if you want to find continued success, then you need to have momentum. Never forget how important momentum is. Once you have it, hold on to it. If you don't, it can be impossible to get back.

Momentum takes time to build. Whether it is for a single project or your entire brand, momentum doesn't just happen overnight. It takes work and effort, but once you have it and once you are on that upswing, do whatever you can in order to hold on to it. The worst thing you can do is get comfortable and complacent. Don't convince yourself that you can start coasting once momentum is on your side; you can't. When you have momentum on your side, it is time to start working even harder.

If you do lose your momentum, it is going to be even harder to get it back than it was to establish it in the first place. If you lose your momentum, you should be prepared to work twice as hard to get it back. This is why you should always be on point, when momentum is on your side. And trust me, you will be able to tell when momentum is on your side.

If you are, then you can achieve extraordinary things and take your company to a whole new level in a shorter period of time. Momentum is a really powerful thing, you just need to be willing to treat it like the precious commodity that it is. Make the most of the time that you have when momentum is on your side and you will make leaps and bounds ahead of others in your field.

9. Be Ready to Make Sacrifices

This is something that I tell every aspiring entrepreneur, especially young entrepreneurs, yet it is something that I feel most people don't take seriously at first. This was a hard lesson for me to learn because I was so young when I started my first company. I knew I was willing to work hard and that I would be willing to give things up to find success, but I had no idea what types of sacrifices I would really need to make.

While most kids my age were out partying until the wee hours of the morning or living life without a care in the world, I was working. I had to. Even when I didn't want to, I had to dedicate the time to my company or I knew it would falter. I had to sacrifice my hobbies, a social life and time with my family at times when I didn't want to, but it paid off.

You won't have to sacrifice everything. There is a great deal of importance that comes with a healthy work-life balance, but you are going to need to sacrifice a lot of your free time. In fact, you may be surprised by how much free time you really had when it's time to sacrifice most of it. Whether this is personal time, television time, sleep time or social time, whatever it may be, you are going to need to come back.

The first and most important thing that every new entrepreneur needs to realize is that there is a price to pay for success. It doesn't come easy and it doesn't come free. You need to want it badly enough and you need to be willing to pay that price if you want to find the success that comes with it.

This is not a fun part of being an entrepreneur. In fact, many people find it to be the worst part. However, this is why everyone in the world isn't their own boss. This is why most people can't hack it as entrepreneurs. It isn't easy and not everyone has the strength to sacrifice their free time in order to be successful. Before you really invest all of your time and money into a new business venture, you need to be able to ask yourself if *you* are the type of person that can sacrifice for the betterment of your business.

10. Attend Every Event Possible

When just starting out as an entrepreneur, chances are you are going to hear the phrase "network, network, network," all of the time. While it is a rather over-shared piece of advice, it is one that should never be overlooked. When you are getting started you need to attend every event possible, especially in the beginning.

If there is an opportunity for you to engage in a relative networking experience, then jump on it. This is especially true for in-person networking. While online professional networking does have its place and time, there is nothing that compares to in person networking.

Look up all the major conferences in your industry, and attend them all if you can. Yes, they can be expensive, but they are worth the investment. While you are there, use the cost as a way to motivate yourself to get the most out of the conference. Attending and paying the entrance fee is only half of the battle. You need to take advantage of the opportunities in front of you when you are at these conferences. If you sit in the corner and don't talk to anyone the entire time, you are wasting your opportunity.

Meet as many people as you can and start building relationships with everyone you meet. The key is to build these relationships before you need them. Don't go around and focus only on people that can help you right now. You never know who may be an asset to you in the future.

If you can become an excellent networker, your company will start to take off and you will start building a solid foundation for your business. After all, as I have said before, you can't build a truly successful company without the help of others.

An excellent networker, doesn't just take any opportunity they can to build connections, they look for how they can add value to others whenever they meet a person. You should never meet someone and expect them to do you a favor or bring value to your professional endeavors, before you bring value to them. However, if you can do something for someone else right away, you never know when they may be able to come up big and return the favor.

11. Travel the World

This is advice that I give and have become known for giving in many articles that I write and speeches that I give. After so much emphasis on networking, sales and giving up free time, traveling the world may not seem like the most obvious lesson to make my list, but it is an important one. If you can, travel the world as much as possible.

I want you to think about *why* you became an entrepreneur in the first place. What were your goals? For so many entrepreneurs today, freedom is one of the big goals and big motivating factors in being an entrepreneur. This includes financial freedom and eventually, the freedom to manage your own time and make your own schedule.

Use that freedom wisely once you have it. It may take you a while to get there, but once you do, I highly recommend that you travel as often and as widely as you can. Pick as many different places as you can imagine and diversify your list of "must-see" travel destinations. Visit Asia, Europe, exotic countries most people haven't heard of. Go north, and south. Visit monuments and attractions and take the time to get to know the locals. Do as much traveling as you can, as it will truly pay off for you in the end.

Yes, traveling is a great way to unwind, relax and refresh, but traveling the world is about more than that.

The education and experiences that you will gain from other cultures and environments is invaluable. You can't learn this in a conference and you can't pick it up in a book. It is something that you can only learn by truly immersing yourself in a different culture. I promise you this insight and experience will not only make you a better, more well-rounded person, but it will make you a better entrepreneur.

12. Track and Measure Everything

This is something that will take time to master, but it is a habit that every entrepreneur should have. Peter Drucker put it best when he simply stated "what's measured, improves." If you want your company to grow and if you want to improve, then you need to start measuring everything.

I talk a great deal about goal setting in this book, because I believe that goal setting is the foundation of entrepreneurial success. When it comes to setting any goal one of the first things it needs to be is measurable. If you can't measure a goal or your progress towards a goal, you will never know if you are truly going in the right direction.

Everything about your company that you want to improve should be tracked and measured. This doesn't just include your big goals, and it doesn't just include things inside the office. If you have a goal in your personal life, start tracking it. If you want to see how much money you are making every hour, start tracking it. If you want to know how many minutes you are wasting scrolling through Facebook on a given day, start tracking it.

Start by writing out what it is that you are planning on tracking and then identify the most important and most relevant metric for measuring improvement in that area. Once you have this, start tracking it every single day. It may seem monotonous, but it is the best way to see where you are going and to get the motivation that you need when it comes to tracking the progress you have made so far.

13. Invest in Yourself

There is no denying that starting a company will require you to make some pretty significant investments. However, when it comes to investing in your future as an entrepreneur, one of the best things you can do is to invest in yourself. There is no better place to put your money.

Don't hesitate to invest in your own education. Even if you can invest five percent of your annual income in your education every year, the returns you will receive can easily be 10-fold. It may not happen overnight, but you will see a great return on investment if you are just willing to put just this much into your education.

Continuous learning is imperative to your success as an entrepreneur. No matter how far you come or how much money you make, you should never be done learning. No entrepreneur knows everything and no entrepreneur should ever be done learning.

You should always be finding new classes to take, books to read, and seminars to attend to constantly continue your education. The worst thing you can do as an entrepreneur is to stop learning. If you dedicate time and money to educating yourself, you are dedicating time and money towards a more successful future.

14. Become a Public Speaker

If you ask most people what their biggest fears are, chances are public speaking is near the top of the list. While your day to day responsibilities as an entrepreneur may not require you stand up and deliver a 40-minute speech in front of a 1,000-person crowd, you still need to work on your public speaking skills.

If you are comfortable with speaking in front of crowds of people, you are naturally going to become more confident in speaking in front of others. This will only help you when it comes to finding new clients and networking yourself.

How do you practice your public speaking skills? Seize as many opportunities as you can to speak at industry conferences whenever possible. Even if it is a small room or a non-paying gig, you need to start somewhere and you need to start delivering as many speeches as possible.

This is a great way for you to gain exposure and to put your face out in front of others in your industry. This is one of the best ways to start branding yourself and start creating a strong reputation for yourself as an entrepreneur and for your company.

With public speaking gigs, you can start acquiring new clients, find partners and investors, and most importantly start opening up doors for countless opportunities. If you want to give yourself the best chance for success in the future and the most opportunities possible, then public speaking is by far one of the most effective ways to do so.

While I have learned countless lessons throughout my own journey as an entrepreneur, I truly believe that these 15 lessons are some of the most pertinent in shaping my own career and my own success in this industry.

CHAPTER 8

HOW TO PROMOTE YOURSELF

People don't buy what you do, they buy why you do it. – Simon Sinek

There are so many entrepreneurs today who believe in the misconceived notion that all they need in order to make their company a success in the right idea. While a great idea can be a strong foundation for any company, it isn't everything. You need more than just an idea in order to make a company successful. An idea on its own is nothing, you need the right entrepreneur behind that idea in order to execute this idea.

This means that in order for your business venture to be successful, you need to do more than just promote the idea at the base of your company, you need to be able to promote yourself as the entrepreneur driving your organization. The difference between a good idea for a company and a successful organization lies in the abilities of the entrepreneur.

This is why it is so important to be able to promote *yourself* as an entrepreneur. Even if self-promotion doesn't come naturally to you, it is essential that you are able to put yourself out there and sell yourself as an entrepreneur. If you want to have the most successful company possible, you need to immediately accept that you are going to need to sell yourself as a brand and as a person, just as much as you sell your company.

It may be uncomfortable at first, but these are some of the best ways to start promoting yourself as the type of entrepreneur that will take your company to the next level. I have broken up my most basic self-promotion strategy into ten key tips. Apply these to your efforts and really put some extra energy into promoting yourself outside of your business, and you can start seeing more growth and more reputability in your organization.

Know Who You Are

If you don't know who you are not only as a person but as an entrepreneur, then there is no point in trying to promote yourself; your efforts will prove to be futile. You need to understand who you are as a brand. You are completely unique and aren't the same as any other entrepreneur out there. But what does that mean? If you can understand yourself as a brand and you are clear on who you are, then your promotional messages are going to be clear as well.

Simply put, the better you understand yourself as a brand, the easier everything else in terms of your promotional efforts is going to be. You are your own brand, and above all things people are going to buy other people, not a list of qualifications, so make sure that you have formed a solid brand identity for yourself before you start promoting yourself as a person.

Create a Clear Thesis Statement For Yourself

When you were in school and had to create a thesis statement for your papers, the goal was to make one clear and concise sentence or idea that embodied everything you were going to try to prove in your paper. I want you to do the same thing about your identity, before you go any farther in terms of promotional activities.

If you want to build a sense of trust among your audience then you need to show them how you are solving a problem that may be in their lives or what you are going to do to them. Be direct. Craft a thesis statement for yourself that talks about *what* you are going to do and highlights what the benefits are of working with you.

Remember, people want to know what's in it for them, so before you start promoting yourself to people you need to be able to highlight what the benefits are of working with you and trusting you. Let people know what *they* will get out of working with your company.

Everything else you do in terms of promoting yourself is the rest of your research, the supporting information that will prove *why* these things are true. However, you still need to have a clear statement at the heart of your efforts.

Create the Right Reputation

From the moment that you start promoting yourself as an entrepreneur, you need to accept the idea that your personal life is now going to become public. With this in mind, one of your biggest areas of focus needs to be on creating the right reputation for yourself.

Your reputation is the best asset that you have, so make sure that you are giving it the right amount of attention and that you don't tarnish the good reputation that you have. Your title isn't the most important thing standing behind your name, it is what people think of you and whether or not they trust you. Focus on creating a reputation for yourself that you can be proud of, and remember to take extra, preventative steps to make sure that your reputation does not get tarnished.

One of the many ways that you can do this is to make sure that you keep your social media accounts clean. Remember, what you do in your personal life can have a serious effect on your professional one. The right social media efforts can build up your personal brand and help you create the image you want, but the wrong posts can do far more damage than good in a very short amount of time.

Work with the Media

If you want to get a positive image out there and really solidify your reputation as one of the industry's leading entrepreneurs, then one of the best ways that you can get the word out there and really establish yourself as an authority, is to work with the media.

If you can build a positive presence in the media, then it is going to take you so far in today's market. The right media presence will help put you in touch with the right people, it will help establish credibility and it can lead to new opportunities. Put yourself out there and send press releases, offer yourself up for quotes and try to get media coverage on every event that you do. Your efforts will go a long way in helping you get that positive recognition you have been looking for.

Network, Network, Network

I know this is one of those pieces of advice that is over-prescribed, but it is something worth mentioning. I hammer this idea into the minds of every entrepreneur that I meet, because I truly believe that networking is one of the best things you can do to grow your company. The more connections that you have, the higher your chances of success are going to be.

Promoting yourself is not all about the big picture and putting your face out there in front of big crowds, many times, the one-on-one interactions and connections are just as important.

In today's market, it is less about *what* you know and more about *how* you know. We live in a very social economy so take advantage of that opportunity and get out and connect with as many people as possible. The more connections the better, but in the end, all you need is one person in order to make all of the difference in your success as an entrepreneur.

Just one connection, one investor, one business partner, or even one client can make all of the difference in your company so never forget about getting out there, making connections and networking with others in the industry.

Know Who You Are Promoting To

So many people in marketing talk about your "target market" of consumers. While it is an overused term, it is something that is so important not only when marketing a product, but when marketing yourself. If you are trying to promote yourself as an entrepreneur, then you need to know who you are promoting to.

You need to know your market, and you need to know them well. The better you understand them, the better your results will be. If you have a vague understanding of who it is that you are talking to, you will only get vague results in return.

It can seem like a big time commitment, but you really need to put in the work and do the research to understand who your target market of clients really is. Know who these individuals are. What do they need from you? Use this information to your advantage and your promotional efforts will be much more efficient.

Be Accountable

I've already talked about the importance of your reputation and that people are looking for someone that they can trust and rely on. This is why it is so important that you are being accountable for everything that you do and everything that happens with your company. This will show people that you are trustworthy, which is one of the most valuable assets that any entrepreneur can have while they are trying to promote themselves.

Take charge of your life and what you are looking to accomplish as an entrepreneur. If you are accountable for your own success and always looking to learn and grow, then you are never going to get anywhere. Accountability will not only help you in terms of promotion but it can be that driving force that you need to get yourself motivated to get out there and promote yourself.

Focus on Your Accomplishments

I talk to so many young entrepreneurs that struggle with self-promotion because they don't think that they have enough experience. So many people believe that you need to have a certain amount of experience to your name to be worthy of being promoted in the market or worthy of having a certain amount of success and respect.

Forget about experience or the number of years or even hours you have to your name as an entrepreneur. Instead focus on your accomplishments. Focus on the milestones you have completed and where you have gotten thus far in your efforts, no matter how small your successes are. Help the public see the value that you bring and the work ethic that you have. It is much more important than the number of years you have been in the business.

Always Present Yourself as an Expert

If you want to start growing your business then you need to start promoting yourself as an expert. You don't need to be just another entrepreneur, you need to be the *best* entrepreneur in your field. No one is going to invest in a business that *might* do OK, they are going to invest in a business that they think is going to succeed.

You need to constantly be positioning yourself as an expert and as someone that is going to succeed. After all, you are what is going to make your business succeed. Always use this framework with anything you do in self-promotion. It will only help solidify your strong reputation and the strong reputation of your company.

Let Go of Your Fears

If there is one thing that can get in the way of any person's efforts to self-promote, it is fear and uncertainty. If you want to really start getting the attention you have been looking for, then you need to let go of your fears and apprehension.

You also need to realize when your fears are masking your ability to promote yourself. If you are afraid of putting yourself out there, of judgement or of failure it can really get in your way when it comes to your self-promotion efforts. You need to be honest with yourself about these apprehensions and whether or not they are preventing you from promoting yourself to the best of your ability. These fears need to be addressed if you want to get the most out of your efforts.

Keep these ten tips in mind when it comes to self-promotion. While it may not come naturally to everyone, the right self-promoting efforts can go a long way in help you not only build your personal brand but build your company's strong reputation as well.

CHAPTER 9

ATTITUDE SEPARATES WINNERS FROM LOSERS

People may hear your words, but they feel your attitude. – John C. Maxwell

I have spent a great deal of time in this book talking about some of the hands-on and more tactical approaches to entrepreneurship that I believe can help any person just getting started in the industry. However, I want to take some time and talk about attitude. Your attitude is one of the most important assets that you have working to your advantage. One of the most difficult parts of talking about attitude is the idea of *changing* that attitude.

For the most part, your attitude is something that comes naturally. It is up to you to make changes and tweaks to your outlook so you can change your attitude. Drastically changing your outlook and perception of things is no easy undertaking and it will take some work. However, if you are willing to make the effort to change your attitude, the results may shock you.

If there is one summarizing concept I have gathered from my years in working with entrepreneurs, it is that their attitudes truly have an impact on their success. If there is one thing that can actually separate the winners from the losers in the world of entrepreneurship, it is absolutely their attitudes.

If it was easy to simply have a great attitude, then everyone would have one and everyone would be a "winner" so to speak. This is why it is so important that you are willing to put in the extra effort in order to really change your attitude for the better. When it comes to making these changes, I have a few tips that can help anyone adopt that "winning" mindset they need in order to separate themselves from other entrepreneurs in the pack.

Staying Positive

The first and most important component of a good attitude is positivity. For you to truly have a positive attitude, you not only need to get in a positive mindset every day, but you need to be able to stay positive through difficult situations as well. This is actually much harder than it seems, but there are a few things that you can start doing that will help you stay positive, even through all of the ups and downs that can come with a career as an entrepreneur.

Express gratitude for the things that are going well in your life. There are going to be times where life gets hard and it becomes difficult to stay positive. In these times, make sure to focus on the good things you have in life, it can really help put things in perspective.

Start saying positive affirmations. This is something that I encourage every person to do. If you want to be positive every day, say positive affirmations to yourself every day. These messages needs to be about who you are and what you are able to do with your life. Trust me, the more often you hear positive messages like this, the more you will start to believe it. Repeat your affirmations every day, even if that affirmation is "I am improving as an entrepreneur every day." And it will start to completely reverse your negative mindset.

Call yourself out. If you want to be able to stay positive even when things aren't going well, then you need to start training yourself to stay positive even when your brain naturally wants to think negative. You need to think of your own way to catch yourself and your own way to "punish" yourself for thinking negatively, even if it is just writing in your planner "today I had negative thoughts." Think of this as the same concept as putting a dollar in the swear jar. The more you retrain your mind to avoid negative thoughts the less negativity will infiltrate your brain.

These are three of the most effective ways to stay positive and to maintain a positive attitude no matter what challenges may come your way.

Avoiding Scarcity Mindset

A scarcity mindset is a mindset based on fear and it is one that can ultimately bring a great deal of negativity into your life and your attitude. The idea is that you believe there is never enough of something in your life and that there is nothing you can do about it. People who have a scarcity mindset often use words like "I can't" or "I don't have." If you think you don't have enough money and will never have enough money, then you are living in a scarcity mindset.

Think of a scarcity mindset like thinking about the world as though it was a pie and that there is only one pie out there. If someone gets a big piece of the pie, then it means there is less available for everyone else. This is not how the world works, but there are many people that think that way. "If I don't spend my money now, someone will take it." "If I don't party when I'm young, I'll never do it."

This is such a common way of thinking, but it is such a negative way of thinking and is filled with limitations. It does not allow you to look at the big picture, it breeds sadness and jealousy and it is filled with negativity. It will also hold you back from making the smart choices you need to take your business to the next level. Avoid this mindset at all costs.

If you find yourself falling back on this way of thinking, then start trying to reframe your attitude with a more "abundance" driven mindset. Think "there is plenty out there, there is enough for everyone to find success." This way of thinking allows you to focus more on what *you* can do in order to earn *your* amount of success. It correlates hard work, decision making and action with profits, recognition and success. It is a much more positive and open way of thinking and something that will ultimately impact your attitude as well.

Never Act Out of Desperation or Fear

If you want to maintain the right type of attitude for the world of entrepreneurship, then one of the biggest things that you need to focus on is avoiding acts based on fear or desperation. If you act out of desperation or fear, you are not only likely making poor decisions, but you are telling yourself that fear and desperation can control your life. These are negative thoughts and negative feelings and if you let them be in control of the actions you take, then you are never going to maintain a positive attitude.

There are going to be times in your journey as an entrepreneur where you are going to feel desperate and you are going to want to make decisions that will fix the issue in the short term. Don't be tempted by these quick-fixes. There are also going to be plenty of times when you are scared. Scared about failing, about not paying the bills, about lawsuits, about paying your workers. No matter what it is, you are going to have fear in your life when you are trying to run a business.

When you have fear and desperation driving you, it is easy to panic, and when you are running your own business, panicking is one of the worst things that you can do. If you talk to any successful entrepreneur, chances are one of their best redeeming qualities is that they are able to stay "cool under pressure." In fact, this is a quality that most organizations look for in any leader. Never acting out of fear and desperation and never panicking when things get tough is what is going to separate you from the countless other entrepreneurs who may ultimately succumb to the pressures of this industry.

An entrepreneur with a "winning" attitude is able to stay calm, look at these high-emotion situations with composure and put a more positive spin on it. In these situations, there is typically a positive answer to your problem that isn't driven by fear and desperation. You just need to have the right attitude in order to avoid those tempting feelings and make the right call.

Don't Lose Your Temper

Being an entrepreneur is one of the most emotionally taxing jobs on the planet and unfortunately, many people don't realize this until they get into the thick of it. You are going to be tested each and every day. Things are going to go wrong, people may not pay you, investors may back out, projects may go over budget, all of these things can come at you every day, and chances are they are going to come at you at once.

If you tend to have a temper, then stressful situations like this can set you off. It is so important that you don't lose your temper. It will help you maintain that attitude that you need to have and it will help you keep your positive reputation as an entrepreneur—something I have discussed in great detail in this book. Going off the handle and losing your temper is never going to help you or your business, so you need to learn how to exercise the self-control necessary to keep a calm and composed attitude no matter what comes your way.

For some people, this is as easy as taking a breath or exercising, while for others they may need to engage in some more involved anger management techniques. Either way, your temper needs to be controlled if you are going to make it in any industry and maintain a company that thrives off of its good reputation and its ability to serve its clients.

Never Act Rashly

In entrepreneurship, you need to be able to make smart, calculated decisions that not only better your company in the present, but in the future as well. You aren't just starting a company for short-term success, a company is often a lifelong commitment. Every decision you make as the head of this company can impact its future and your future success.

This is why it is so important to never act rashly. If you are naturally an impulsive person, then it is important that you get these feelings of rash activity under control. If you are tempted to act rashly or make decisions without thinking about them, then you may be putting your future at risk.

Challenge yourself to think through every decision before you make it. This may mean writing down pros and cons lists or simply thinking out loud before making a decision. However, being able to maintain composure when tough decisions need to be made and being able to rationally think multiple sides of a decision through, is what will help you make the smart, composed decisions that you need to in order to stand out from the crowd of entrepreneurs.

Rash decision making isn't something that people normally contribute to a good or bad attitude, but it can actually be a very negative way of thinking and one that ultimately contributes to a negative outcome for your company. An entrepreneur with the right attitude, knows the importance of their decisions and the importance of seeing things from multiple angles and will ultimately continue to possess the "winning" attitude that they need.

One of the most challenging components of entre-preneurship, especially for first-time entrepreneurs has to be finding that way to separate yourself from others in the industry and to really help make your own business and your own efforts stand out from the crowd. One of the best ways to do this is with your attitude. There are so many entrepreneurs out there who are willing to put in the hours, work hard, read eBooks and everything in between. However, in this challenging business, there are very few who can continue to adopt a positive attitude throughout the entire process. Work on your positive attitude until it becomes part of your everyday life and you will be astounded by the difference it makes and how far ahead it can get you.

RECOMMENDED READING

Your learning should not stop here. Below is a list of the books that have made a tremendous impact on my life and business. I highly recommend picking them up.

The Compound Effect, Darren Hardy

The Monk Who Sold His Ferrari, Robin Sharma

The Greatness Guide, Robin Sharma

Leading an Inspired Life, Jim Rohn

Traction, Gino Wickman

The Success Principles, Jack Canfield

The Slight Edge, Jeff Olson

The 15 Invaluable Laws of Growth, John C. Maxwell

Today Matters, John C. Maxwell

Driven, Robert Herjavec

Relentless, Tim S. Grover

Swim with the Sharks Without Getting Eaten Alive, Harvey Mackay

The Self-made Billionaire Effect, John Sviokla and Mitch Cohen

The Alliance, Reid Hoffman

No Limits, John C. Maxwell

The Data Driven Marketing Agency, Roger Bryan

Grit, Angela Duckworth

Momentum, Shama Hyder

Be Obsessed or Be Average, Grant Cardone

Rocket Fuel, Gino Wickman & Mark C. Winters

Matter, Peter Sheahan & Julie Williamson

The Obstacle is the Way, Ryan Holiday

Tools of Titans, Tim Ferriss

LIFE VISION OUTLINE

The first step in transforming any area of your life is knowing exactly how you want that transformation to look and being able to visualize it clearly within your mind. The only way to get to that level of specificity and clarity is by putting a pen to paper. Using the allotted spaces below, write out and describe in exact detail, what your ideal life would look like in each of the listed areas. Be as specific as you can in what you have, what you are feeling and what your experiences are like.

Once you've completed this, review it often to keep yourself focused on your greater vision. You will also use this vision to help with setting your goals in the next exercise.

Business/Career: In your ideal life, what does your business or career look like? What do you do, what is your title, how much money are you earning, what kind of impact are you making, who do you do business with and associate with, what recognitions have you received?

Finances: What do your finances look like? How much money do you earn, what is your net worth, how much money do you have saved, how much money do you have invested and where, how much money do you contribute to charity, what is your mindset about money?

Family/Relationships: What does your family life look like?

Health/Fitness: What is your health and level of fitness like?

Spirituality: What does your spiritual life look like?

Lifestyle: What is your lifestyle like? Where do you travel, what do you do in your free time, what hobbies/interests do you enjoy?

Mental/Mindset: What does your personal growth look like? What areas and skills do you want to improve your knowledge in?

GOAL ACTION SHEET

This exercise is designed to help you start taking immediate action on any sized goal. Especially with large goals, the challenge of the task in front of you can appear daunting and overwhelming, preventing you from taking action. By following the exercise below, you will be able to identify tasks that you can start today in order to move you in the direction of your goal. Remember, you don't need to see the whole staircase to take the first step. The important thing is to identify small steps you can take now and then immediately take them.

Identify Your Goal:

Take Action: Below list 25 actions you can take right now in order to reach your goal. Be as specific as possible in the steps you can take. This is not as simple as it looks. The first 10 are easy but as you get closer to 20 and 25, you will be forced to get creative.

1.

2.

3.

4.

5.

6.

7.

8.

9.

10.

11.

12.

13.

14.

15.

16.

17.

18.

19.

20.

21.

22.

23.

24.

25.

Next Steps:

Start taking action on these items immediately, one at a time until your goal is reached.

ABOUT
RICHARD LORENZEN

Richard Lorenzen is one of the most influential entrepreneurs in America and a top online influencer. Born as the child of a fireman and a journalist in Long Island, New York, Richard's interest in entrepreneurship and drive to achieve led him to start his first online business venture at the age of 15. His early dive into the emerging space of internet marketing allowed him to build a fast-growing online agency which became a launch pad for his career. Now at the age of 25, Richard has been named by Inc. Magazine as one of the top inspiring entrepreneurs of 2017, Entrepreneur Magazine as one of the top 50 people in digital marketing and by Inc. Magazine as one of top eight entrepreneurs on Twitter. LinkedIn named him one of the top millennial influencers of 2016.

As a serial entrepreneur and investor, Richard has built and sold multiple online media properties. Today, he is the founder and CEO of Fifth Avenue Brands, a public relations and digital media firm headquartered in New York. He is a member of the Young Entrepreneur Council, an invite-only organization for the top entrepreneurs in America, and a founding member of the Forbes Agency Council.

Richard now spends time speaking to audiences ranging from high school students to CEOs about entrepreneurship. His mission is to share his expertise and experience to empower and inspire other young people to become entrepreneurs and to strive for their potential.

Follow Richard on Instagram: @RichardLorenzen

For more information, www.richardlorenzen.com

75209193R00082

Made in the USA
Columbia, SC
14 August 2017